100 Signs You Might Be Irish

BY MULTI-MILLION-BOOK-SELLING AUTHOR
BRIAN P. CLEARY

D1520230

FAB-U-LIST-BOOKS

FOREWORD

Cheers! With a name like Brian Patrick Cleary, you probably already know where my ancestors come from. And one look at the younger me—a freckled, reddish-haired kid with skin the color of Xerox paper—would remove any lingering doubt. Names like John Reedy and Brigid Reape dotted our family Bible, and my own last name, Cleary, is from the Gaelic Ó Cléirigh or Mac Cleirigh, meaning descendant or son of cleric or clerk.

These "clerks" were often the people recording the town's births and deaths, and more than 1,000 years ago, anyone who could read and write was like the valedictorian of the village.

As a child, my father had five Patricks in his small home in East Cleveland, Ohio. There was Big Pat, Little Pat, Paddy (Big Pat's father, Little Pat's grandpa), along with my grandma's brother from Ireland, Pat Reape (always called by first-and-last name), and an Irish immigrant laborer who rented a room in their home, known as "Plain Pat."

When my father came along, my grandma wisely named him Mike.

While each of these observations won't be true for all sons and daughters of Erin, I'm sure the Irish will find a wee bit of truth in these 100 traits that make us who we are. Slàinte!

Brian P. Cleary

1.

Your favorite moisturizer, foundation, aftershave, or accessory is sunscreen.

2.

You know two unrelated people named Pat Sweeney.

3.

Non-Irish people are stubborn, pigheaded and willful.
You are persistent, steadfast and tenacious.

4.

You laugh when you're at wakes…

5.

…and cry when you're at weddings.

6.

You can charm the pants off a mannequin.

7.

A family member in the last 3 generations was named Mary.

8.

You believe that all
of the world's ills
can be cured with
a nice cup o' tea…

9.

…or a touch of whiskey.

10.

You own an item that others call a vegetable peeler that you use exclusively on potatoes.

11.

You have talked your way into
and out of a wee bit o' trouble
in your time.

12.

You can't make a long story short.

13.

You refer to Alcoholics
Anonymous as simply,
"The Program."

14.

If there's a book, poem, or a play—even a musical—about death, you're in.

15.

Notre Dame is your Harvard.

16.

You've heard old-timey relatives use the words amadán, simpleton and "ee-jit."

17.

Your cuisine has always included boiled food.

18.

Other people get drunk. You get philosophical and poetic.

19.

Someone in your clan is a redhead.

20.

You have at least two relatives
who haven't spoken in years.

21.

You've seen "The Quiet Man" at
least five times.

22.

You can correctly pronounce the word "shillelagh."

23.

You've eaten something your mother cooked and weren't entirely sure what it was.

24.

You own at least two songs by
the Pogues, and Elvis Costello.

25.

…and two more by Van Morrison and U2.

26.

You have a male relative who lived with his "ma" till age 54.

27.

You may forget things like birthdays or where you put your keys, but you remember with great accuracy every person who has ever slighted, snubbed or otherwise wronged you.

28.

To you, "tan" is a color,
not an activity.

29.

Attending wakes is NOT optional.

30.

You can tell the difference
between Canadian Club and
Jameson by sniffing the cap.

31.

You know at least two lines to "Danny Boy."

32.

…and will sing it out loud when you're feeling philosophical and poetic.

33.

You have an ancestor who was a firefighter…

34.

...or a railroad worker...

35.

. . .or a priest.

36.

Your favorite Beatle is Paul because he wrote, "Give Ireland Back to the Irish."

37.

You have an Aunt Peggy…

38.

…and an Uncle Danny.

39.

If you're buying something new, from a car to a t-shirt, green seems like a pretty good color choice.

40.

You have a relative who was taught by the nuns.

41.

You know a guy named Murphy who goes by "Murph."

42.

You have an uncle who wears white socks with a suit.

43.

You have two friends who have
at least eight siblings each.

44.

…and when they name them, it's always fast and in birth order.

45.

From a tattoo to a necklace to a ring, you have something claddagh.

46.

Scandinavians and Norwegians comment about how fair your skin is.

47.

You know how to pronounce Slainte!

48.

Despite the many scholarly books
stating it as fact, you refuse to
believe that St. Patrick was,
in fact, English.

49.

If there were a corned-beef-and-cabbage pizza available, you'd at least give it a try.

50.

You were not a lifeguard in high school.

51.

You have relatives named Mary Grace, Mary Rose, or Mary Pat.

52.

...or perhaps all three.

53.

You've at least attempted
to read James Joyce, Yeats
or Oscar Wilde…

54.

… if not, you've watched "The Departed," "Mystic River," and "The Brothers McMullen.

55.

… if not, then, "Waking Ned Divine," "Angela's Ashes" and "The Commitments."

56.

You had an older relative who said, "Jesus, Mary and Joseph!" out of frustration.

57.

That same relative had a picture
of JFK prominently displayed
somewhere.

58.

What others may call a violin, you call a fiddle.

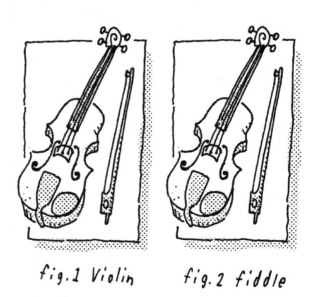

fig.1 Violin   fig.2 fiddle

59.

You refer to geographical locations by "parish."

60.

Your father gave directions with taverns as landmarks.

61.

Your mother works in "guilt" the way other artists work in watercolor or sculpture.

62.

If someone is speaking
in a brogue, you can translate
for your non-Irish friends.

63.

You find the sound of bagpipes
to be soothing.

64.

You can laugh your way through
most of life's difficulties.

65.

You never let the truth interfere with a good story.

66.

You have a wee bit
of the devil in you.

67.

You have a drawer with holy cards from memorial services you attended.

68.

You ditched school or work
at least once to attend a
St. Patrick's Day parade.

69.

You have wondered if the name Obama was missing an apostrophe.

70.

You had to sit through somebody's Irish step dance recital at some point.

71.

...if not, then somebody had to
sit through yours.

72.

If you're like 5% English, you just don't bring that up when talking about your ethnicity.

73.

You once had freckles.

74.

If you're a man, your mother thought that "no girl was good enough" for her boy.

75.

Statistically, your eyes are likely to be blue.

76.

Your thoughts occasionally go dark.

77.

You laugh at completely inappropriate times.

78.

Bossy women are found on both sides of your family.

79.

Your blood type is Guinness.

80.

Whether you've worn it or not,
you've owned a tweed cap.

81.

You have a relative who was in a union.

82.

Someone in your family's middle name is Marie.

83.

You have a vague sense of arrogance about your ethnicity.

84.

There are no professional chefs in your family.

85.

You have had relatives in the front seat of a squad car...

86.

...and the back.

87.

You like a bit of soda bread with your tea.

88.

The daily obituaries are required reading.

89.

You know how to correctly pronounce at least one of the following: bodhran, craic, and Erin go bragh.

90.

You've received more than one
greeting card with the words
"May the road rise up
vto meet you..."

91.

You know most of the lyrics to
Too-Ra-Loo-Ra-Loo-Ral,
or Danny Boy…

92.

...and even if you don't, that doesn't stop you from singing it.

93.

Through sun exposure, you have burned, blistered, and hoped to get enough freckles to merge and look like a suntan.

94.

You keep a mental list of big-name actors who suck at doing an Irish accent.

95.

You believe in God, but you also believe in leprechauns, fairies, banshees, changelings, gnomes, Druids, and pots of gold.

96.

You think that wine, beer–even water–tastes better when sipped from Waterford crystal.

97.

The weather is 51 degrees, it's wet underfoot, with gray skies above, and you describe the weather as "lovely."

98.

Someone asks you, "Who's better, Muhammad Ali or Rocky Marciano?" and you answer, "John L. Sullivan."

99.

Your grandmother's recipe for Irish stew may have called for a wee bit of ale or wine.

100.

The phrase "Fighting Irish" could be the newspaper headline from your latest Thanksgiving, Christmas or family reunion.

ABOUT THE AUTHOR:

American humorist and poet, Brian P. Cleary, was born in Lakewood, Ohio, the third oldest of nine children. He "grew up" in one of the 5 largest creative divisions in the world, where he has put words in the mouths of Dolly Parton, William Shatner, Kevin Nealon, Michael Bolton, and Smokey Robinson. His "What I've Learned" pieces have appeared in Esquire Magazine, and his books of poetry and grammar have sold more than 3 million copies. He has witnessed one of baseball's perfect games, given the Heimlich Maneuver 4 times, and has never had a cup of coffee in his life. Occasionally, he just lists random things about himself with no narrative context.

Made in the USA
Las Vegas, NV
28 February 2022

44733732R00059